Say Hello To Tyto

Learn more about barn owls throughout the book with Tyto's fascinating facts.

Dusk Until Dawn

Where's Volee?

Do you have the ears and eyes of a barn owl? See if you can spot Volee hidden on every picture page.

By Martin Bradley

Thanks to Colin and Val Shawyer of the BOCN, Ashley Smith and Penny Smout at the Hawk Conservancy Trust, Simon Chadwick, Linda Wright Photography, Nick Dixon, Alison Jones and the Bradley family.

This book is in memory of Steve Bradley (my Dad)
"A man who gave us everything and asked for nothing in return"

Ceratopia Books, 2 Solent Road, Dibden Purlieu, SO45 4QG

First published in Great Britain 2014   Text & Illustrations © 2014 Martin Bradley
Martin Bradley has asserted his rights to be identified as author and illustrator of this work under the Copyright, Designs and Patents Act, 1998. All rights reserved.

ISBN 0-9542791-3-1
Printed by John Dollin Printing Services Ltd, Whitchurch, Hampshire

Ceratopia BOOKS

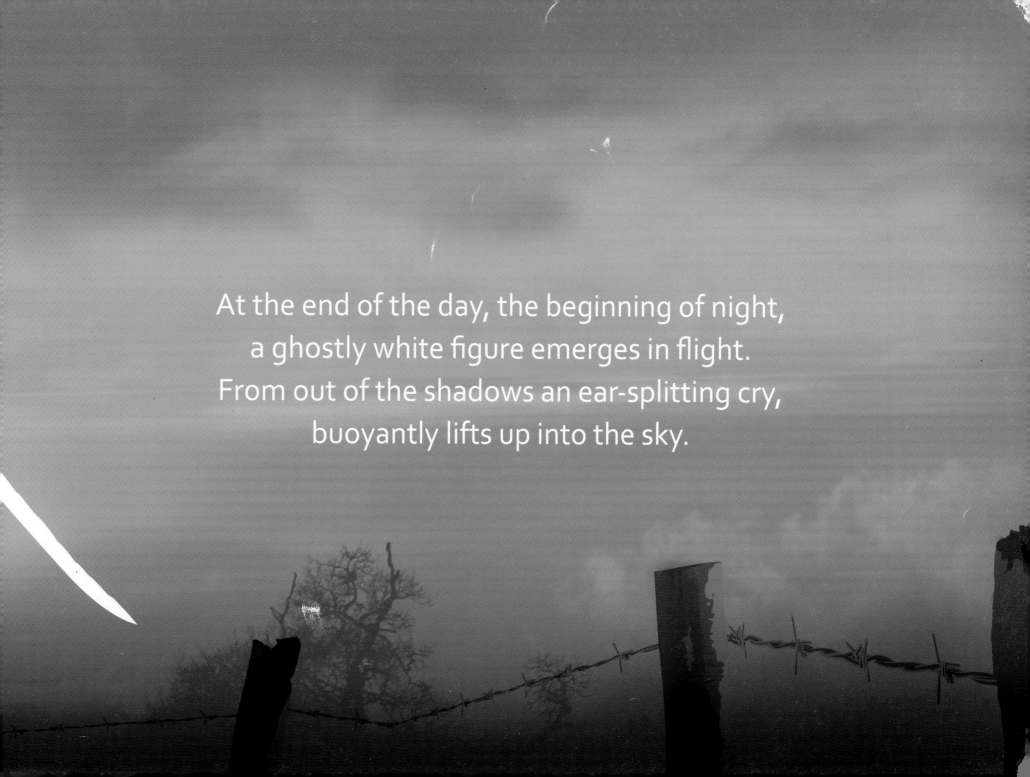

At the end of the day, the beginning of night,
a ghostly white figure emerges in flight.
From out of the shadows an ear-splitting cry,
buoyantly lifts up into the sky.

Crossing the roads and avoiding the lights,
metal monsters below roaring with fright.

The biggest threats and dangers to barn owls are: high speed traffic on the roads; bad weather; loss of habitat causing starvation (not enough food).

Drifting along hedgerows with beauty and grace,
detecting all noises with a heart-shaped face.

twit

twoo

The feathers on a barn owl's face create a disc, which helps trap and
focus sound into the ear openings beneath.
Tawny owls twit-twoo, barn owls have an ear-splitting shriek.

Silently floating, patrolling the ground,
satellite dish receiving all sound.

Barn owl ears are asymmetrical, which means one ear is higher than the other. This helps them pinpoint tiny sounds. The right ear focuses on sounds above whilst the left ear on sounds below. If they were wearing headphones it would look lopsided like this.

Pinpointing target, hovering, head still...

Barn owls have superb hearing and good eyesight.
They can catch prey in total darkness using their hearing alone.

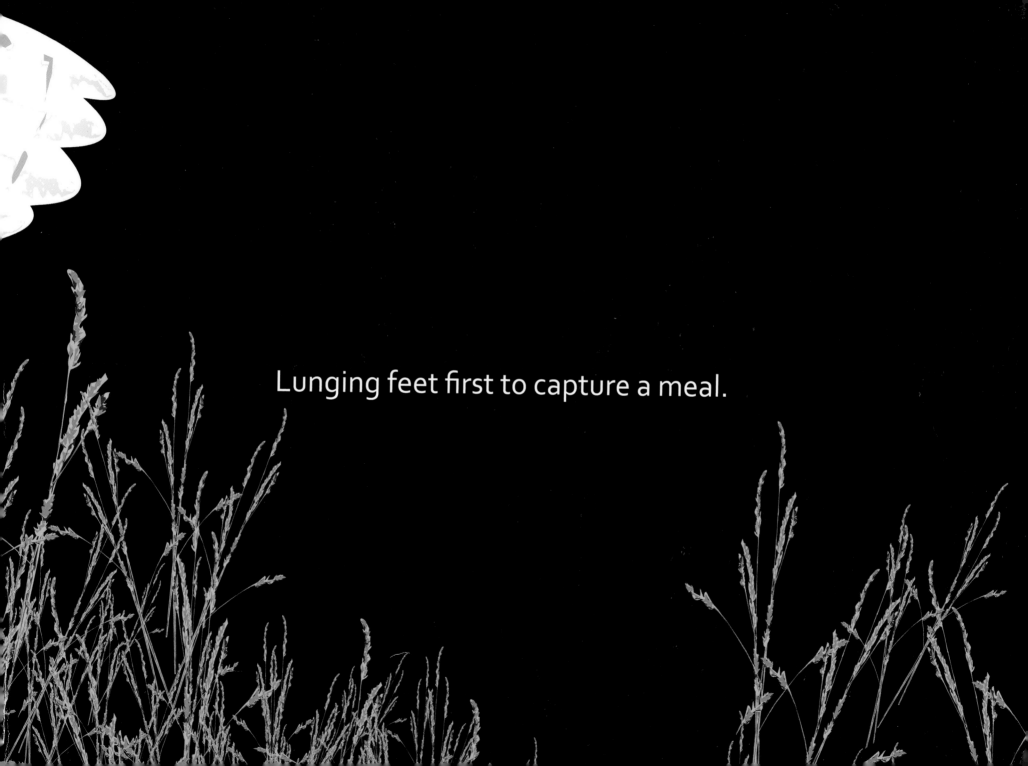

Lunging feet first to capture a meal.

Prey gripped within talons, returns to the farm,
through the broken glass window at the end of the barn.

Barn owls eat mainly small mammals like voles, mice and shrews and, very occasionally, small birds. They have long legs and talons which enable them to catch prey (food) in long grass. Barn owls like to nest in large tree hollows and buildings such as barns and sometimes churches. Just like garden birds, barn owls now rely almost entirely on nestboxes which need to be large and dark inside.

Under the rafters the nestbox in view,
owlets pushing to the front of the queue.

Barn owls begin incubating (keeping warm) each egg as soon as it is laid; normally this occurs at two-day intervals. This means that each chick that hatches is two days older than its brother or sister. If there is not enough food some of the chicks do not always survive.

Dinner is served, a juicy fresh vole,
quickly devoured by swallowing whole.

After eating, owls regurgitate (cough up) indigestible parts of their meal —
the bones and hair of prey. This is called a pellet.
The pellet can provide really good clues as to what an owl has been eating.

Parents set out to hunt once again,
keen to catch food and avoid all the rain.

On average a barn owl requires between two and four small mammals a night to survive. This means that one owl could eat as many as 1460 meals a year, so is dependent on the amount of food available. In years when field voles are scarce or difficult to find, it's bad news for the barn owl.

Hunting deployed from a barbed-wire perch,
rain drops start falling, hampering search.

Barn owls usually hunt by slowly flying back and forth across a patch of rough grassland, listening and looking downwards most of the time. Where suitable perches are available, the "sit and wait" or "post" method of hunting is used.

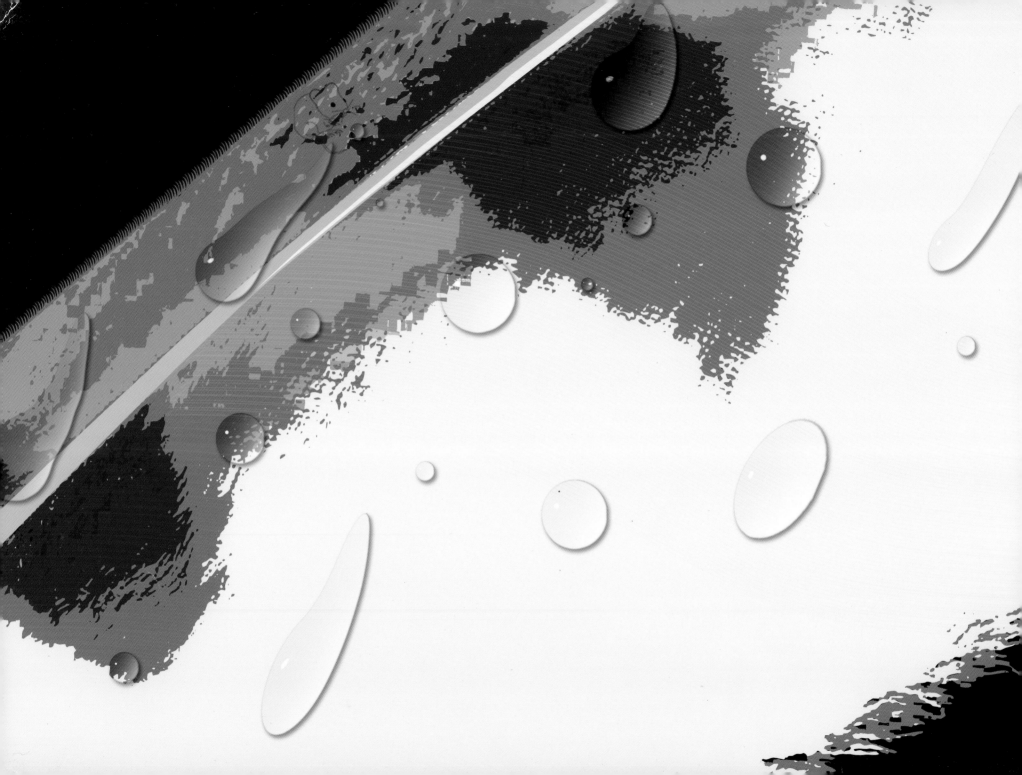

Soft feathered raincoat soaked through to the skin,
in weather like this the barn owl can't win.

Barn owl feathers are very soft, which helps them fly silently.
Unfortunately they are not very waterproof.
They try to avoid hunting in the rain because if they become wet they cannot fly silently.

Back to the barn to shelter from storm,
puffing out feathers to keep nice and warm.

Barn owls do not like bad winters especially when the snow covers the ground because it then becomes difficult to find and catch their prey. It's at times like these that some owls hunt for other prey such as small birds.

Eyes tightly closed and hidden away,
neighbours sing loud for the start of the day.

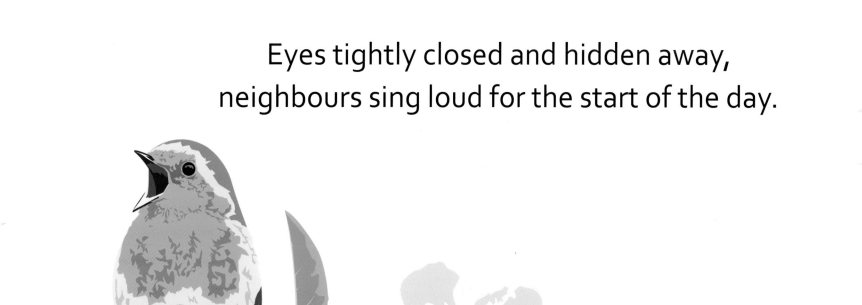

Draw A Barn Owl

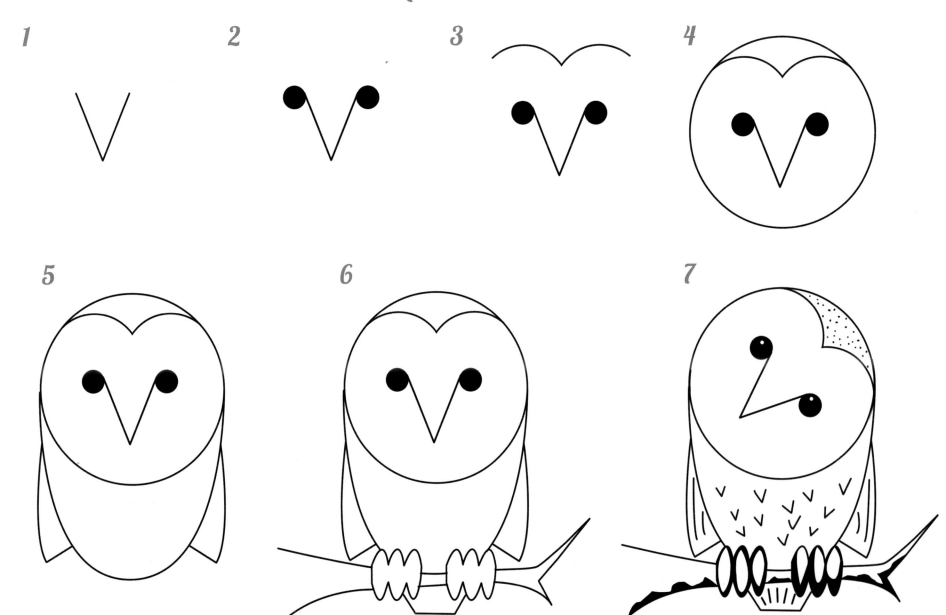

Turn his head to make him look real

Draw A Barn Owl Flying

Draw the face the same as before and add some wings

You have been caught
by a barn owl.

Have your photo taken with an owl
and place it in your book.